Irish Legends on Stage

A collection of plays based on famous Irish legends

Julie Meighan

First published in 2018
by
JemBooks
Cork,
Ireland
dramastartbooks.com

ISBN: 9780993550676

All rights reserved.

No part of this book may be reproduced or utilised in any form or by any electronic, digital or mechanical means, including information storage, photocopying, filming, recording, video recording and retrieval systems, without prior permission in writing from the publisher. The only exception is by a reviewer, who may quote short excerpts in a review. The moral rights of the author have been asserted.

Text Copyright © 2018, Julie Meighan

About the Author

Julie Meighan is a lecturer in Drama in Education at the Cork Institute of Technology. She has taught drama to all age groups and levels. She is the author of the Amazon bestselling *Drama Start: Drama Activities, Plays and Monologues for Young Children (Ages 3-8)* ISBN 978-0956896605, *Drama Start Two: Drama Activities and Plays for Children (Ages 9-12)* ISBN 978-0-9568966-1-2 and *Stage Start: 20 Plays for Children (Ages 3-12)* ISBN 978-0956896629.

Table of Contents

Introduction: 1

The Salmon of Knowledge 2

The King and the Donkey's Ears 5

The Children of Lir 9

The Beggarman 14

Fionn and the Giant 17

Saint Patrick 20

Queen Maebh 26

Fionn and the Dragon 31

The Story of Saint Brendan 34

The Clever Leprechaun and His Pot of Gold 37

Tir na n-Óg 39

Pronunciation of Irish Words: 43

Other Books by the Author: 45

IRISH LEGENDS ON STAGE

A collection of plays based on famous
Irish legends

Julie Meighan
JemBooks

INTRODUCTION:

This delightful collection of plays is based on famous Irish legends. The plays are simple, so it is very easy for children to memorise their lines. The cast list is flexible – more characters can be added, and existing characters can be changed or omitted depending on the size and requirements of the group. The collection includes favourites such as *Saint Patrick*, *The Children of Lir* and *The King with the Donkey's Ears*. The scripts are simple and can be used as performance plays, reader's theatre or just read for enjoyment.

Props/costumes/stage directions:

There is a minimal number of props required to stage these plays. The costumes for all the plays are or can be very simple. For example, the children can just wear a colour that represents their animal, a mask or some face paint. A word of advice: if the children wear masks, make sure they don't cover their mouths as it would make it difficult to hear them speak. All suggestions for stage directions are included in brackets and italics.

I hope you enjoy performing or reading the following plays as much as my drama groups have over the years.

BREAK A LEG!

The Salmon of Knowledge

Characters: Three narrators, Fionn, Mother, Wise Old Woman 1, Wise Old Woman 2, Finéigeas, Salmon.

Narrator 1: Once upon a time, a long, long time ago, there lived a boy called Fionn who lived with his mother.

Narrator 2: He was a very inquisitive little boy. He was always asking questions.

Fionn: Why is the sky blue? Why is the grass green? But why? But why? But why?

Narrator 3: His mother had started to get annoyed by all the questions Fionn asked.

Mother: (*Sighs.*) He never stops asking questions.

Narrator 1: Just then, two wise old women walked by.

Wise Old Woman 1: Whatever is the matter?

Mother: My little boy never stops asking questions. He is driving me mad.

Fionn: Why? Why? Why?

Wise Old Woman 1: We are two wise old women. We will answer all his questions.

Wise Old Woman 2: Let him come live with us.

Mother: Take him, please.

Narrator 2: The two old women took Fionn. He kept asking questions on the way to the old women's cottage.

Fionn: Why? Why? Why?

Wise Old Woman 1: He doesn't stop asking questions.

Wise Old Woman 2: I don't think we know all the answers.

Narrator 1: On their way home, they met Finéigeas. Finéigeas was the wisest man in Ireland.

Finéigeas: Hello ladies, who do we have here?

Wise Old Woman 1: A very inquisitive little boy.

Wise Old Woman 2: We are so wise, but even we don't have enough knowledge to answer all his questions.

Finéigeas: I'm the wisest man in Ireland. He should come with me. I'll answer his questions.

Wise Old Women 1: Please, take him.

Narrator 2: Fionn and Finéigeas lived happily with one another.

Narrator 3: Fionn asked lots of questions and Finéigeas answered them with pleasure.

Fionn: Finéigeas, how can I know everything in the world?

Finéigeas: There is only one way that can happen.

Fionn: Please tell me.

Finéigeas: It is a secret. I couldn't possible tell you.

Narrator 1: Finéigeas and Fionn spent their days fishing and hunting together.

Narrator 2: One day, while they were out fishing, Fionn caught a salmon.

Salmon: Ouch!

Fionn: I caught you at last. Finéigeas, look! I caught this lovely silver salmon.

Narrator 3: Finéigeas was very excited when he saw the fish.

Finéigeas: *(Excitedly.)* You must cook this at once. I will have it for my tea. But, promise me that you will not eat a morsel of it.

(Finéigeas exits.)

Salmon: Well, that's not fair. I'm very big. Finéigeas could share me with you and still have enough left over for his breakfast. Besides, you did catch me.

Fionn: Finéigeas is older and wiser than me, so I will do as he says.

(*While he is cooking the salmon, he burns his thumb on the skin of the salmon.*)

Fionn: Ouch! (*Sucks his thumb.*) That was painful.

(*Finéigeas enters.*)

Fionn: The salmon is ready.

Finéigeas: I hope you didn't eat any of the fish.

Fionn: Of course not.

Finéigeas: Are you sure?

Fionn: Of course, I didn't. (*Sounds not sure.*) I just put my thumb in my mouth when I burnt it on the skin, but I didn't eat any of it. Look at it. (*Fionn shows him the salmon.*)

Finéigeas: Nooo! (*Falls to the floor in desperation.*)

Fionn: What's the matter?

Finéigeas: This is the Salmon of Knowledge. It has all the knowledge in the world. The first person to taste it gains all the knowledge the salmon has.

Fionn: I'm sorry. Here, have the rest of it.

Finéigeas: (*Throws the salmon away.*) I'm not hungry now. It is no good to me. All the knowledge is inside you.

Fionn: But I don't feel any different.

Finéigeas: Put your thumb in your mouth.

Narrator 3: When Fionn put his thumb in his mouth, all the knowledge in the world came rushing in.

Fionn: This is wonderful. A question pops into my head, and I immediately know the answer. What is the square root of pi? (*Thinks for a second.*) I know, it's 1.77245385091. (*Finéigeas hangs his head in disappointment.*)

Narrator 2: Fionn never had to ask anyone a question again.

The King and the Donkey's Ears

Characters: Three narrators, Donal, Mother, King, Servant, Chief Minister, Harp, four courtiers.

Narrator 1: Once upon a time, there was a boy called Donal.

Narrator 2: He wanted to be a barber when he grew up.

Donal: Mother, when I grow up, I want to be a barber.

Mother: Don't be silly. You can't be a barber. Everyone knows what happens to barbers in this land.

Donal: What happens?

Mother: Every year, a barber gets summoned to the King's palace and they are never seen again.

Donal: That won't happen to me.

Narrator 3: Years later, Donal grew up and became a very successful barber.

At the palace:

King: I need a haircut. Summon Donal the barber to the palace at once. I hear he gives a very good haircut.

Servant: Your Majesty, soon there won't be any barbers in the land. Maybe you could stop executing them.

King: Nonsense. Get him for me now. How dare you question my actions. All the barbers who cut my hair are to be executed. That is the rule.

(Servant exits.)

(Servant arrives at Donal's house.)

Servant: You are summoned to the palace to cut the King's hair.

Mother: No! You are not to go Donal.

Donal: I must.

Mother: Stay here. I will go to the palace and talk to the King.

(Mother goes to the palace; she wails and wails.)

Narrator 1: Everyone at the palace put their fingers in their ears.

Narrator 2: However, the king couldn't because he had donkey ears.

(King takes off his crown and shows the audience his donkey ears. He puts the crown back on when he hears someone coming.)

King: Make that noise stop at once. It is driving me insane.

Chief Minister: I can't. She is Donal the barber's mother. She said if you execute her son, she will wail forever.

King: I can't listen to that awful noise. Tell her if she stops immediately, I will let her son live.

(Mother stops wailing and leaves with a smile on her face.)

(Donal enters. He looks nervous.)

King: I will let you live but you must promise not to tell anyone about these…

(The king takes off his crown and shows off his donkey ears.)

(Donal looks very shocked.)

Donal: I promise I will never breathe a word of this to a living soul.

(Donal cuts the king's hair. The king is happy and gives him some money and he puts back on his crown. Donal exits the palace.)

At Donal's house. (Donal is sleeping.)

Narrator 2: Donal tried very hard to keep the king's secret. However, he started to have nightmares about the king's ears.

(Donal starts screaming in his sleep. His mother comes running in and she wakes him.)

Mother: Donal, whatever is the matter? Ever since you came back from the king's palace, you have been having dreadful nightmares.

Donal: The king has a secret. I am the only person who knows. It is driving me mad that I can't tell anyone.

Mother: Tell me.

Donal: I can't. I promised him if he let me live, I wouldn't tell another living soul.

Mother: Well, tell a tree then. It isn't a living soul. There is a big tree down by the lake. You could whisper the secret to it.

Donal: What a clever idea.

Narrator 2: The next day, Donal went for a stroll down by the lake and saw the willow tree. He whispered the king's secret to the tree.

Donal: The king has donkey ears, the king has donkey ears, the king has donkey ears. I feel so much better now that I have gotten that off my chest.

Narrator 3: One day, a harpist passed by the willow tree.

Harpist: What lovely bark. I will cut it down and make a new harp that I will play for the king.

Narrator 1: He made the harp from the tree and when it was ready, he took it to the palace to play for the king.

Narrator 2: As soon as the harpist touched the strings, the harp began to sing by itself.

Harp: The king has donkey ears.

The king has donkey ears.

The king has donkey ears.

Narrator 1: Everyone stared at the king.

King: How dare you. Stop that harp at once. *(His crown falls off and his ears are visible to everyone.)*

Courtier 1: Having donkey ears is not a big deal. Everyone has something they don't like about themselves.

Courtier 2: This is Ireland. It is impossible to keep a secret in this country.

Courtier 3: Now that we all know your secret, you don't have to hide from us anymore. Everyone is different.

Courtier 4: Now that everyone knows, no more barbers must be put to the death.

Narrator 3: Donal was made the royal barber, and his mother was very happy.

Donal: I'm glad I've made you proud.

(Donal and his mother hug.)

THE CHILDREN OF LIR

Characters: Two narrators, Queen, King Lir, Aoife, Aodh, Con, Fiachra, Fionnuala, Druid, Caomhóg.

Narrator 1: Once upon a time, there was a king called Lir. He was married to Queen and they had four children.

Narrator 2: One daughter called Fionnula had three sons called Aodh, Con and Fiachra.

Queen: Come children, let's play.

Children: Yay!

Narrator 3: The queen was very loving, and she sang and played with the children every day.

(Queen hugs them and plays with the them.)

Narrator 1: Unfortunately, she became ill and died. The children and Lir were very sad.

(Shows the queen lying dead and the children crying. Lir is comforting them. They all look very sad.)

King Lir: What shall I do? My children are sad because their mother died. I shall find a new wife for me and a new mother for them.

Narrator 2: He chose a beautiful woman called Aoife to be a loving mother to his children.

King Lir: Aoife, will you marry me.? *(He gets down on one knee to propose.)*

Aoife: Of course, I will.

(King goes to tell the children the good news.)

Aoife: *(Looks at the audience.)* I want to be queen but I'm not a kind-hearted woman. I need to get rid of those annoying children.

(Children enter.)

Aoife: Now let's get one thing straight. I'm not your mother. Don't bother me.

Fiachra: She is very beautiful but very mean.

Aodh: I wish our father never married her.

Con: She is horrible, but we have no choice but to put up with her.

Fionnuala: I wish our mother was still here. *(Fionnuala starts to cry and the other children comfort her.)*

(Lir enters.)

Lir: Children, let's play.

Aoife: He spends more time with those pesky children than he does with me. I need to put a stop to this NOW. Druid, come here.

(Druid enters.)

Aoife: I need you to get rid of those horrible children. *(She points to the children who are playing with their father.)*

Druid: I have a plan. *(Druid whispers in Aoife's ear.)*

Narrator 3: One day, when the children were playing by the lake, Druid crept up behind them. There was a thunderous noise and a flash of time. Druid waved his magic wand.

Narrator 1: The children had disappeared, and in their place, were four beautiful swans.

Fionn: What has happened to you?

Con: You look like a swan. Oh, dear, I look like a swan too.

Fiachra: Aoife, what have you done?

Aodh: We have turned into swans.

Aoife: I want your father all to myself. I've put a spell on you. Now, your father and this kingdom are all mine.

Fionnuala: Turn us back into children now.

Aoife: No. You will be swans for nine hundred years. You will spend three hundred years on this lake, three hundred years on the sea of Moyle and three hundred years on the Isle of Gloria.

Druid: Only the sound of a church bell will make you human again.

(Aoife and Druid cackle with laughter and exit.)

(Lir enters.)

Lir: Children, children, where are you?

Fionnuala: We are over here.

Lir: Where? All I see are four white swans.

Fiachra: We are the swans.

Lir: I don't understand. What happened?

Con: Aoife has placed a terrible spell on us.

Aodh: She has turned us into swans for nine hundred years.

(Aoife enters.)

Lir: Aoife, turn the swans back in to my beautiful children.

Aoife: No, I refuse to turn the swans back into children.

Lir: Then I banish you from my kingdom. *(He pushes her.)* Get out of my land and never come back.

Narrator 1: Lir spent the rest of his life by the lake with his children.

Narrator 2: Eventually, he died. The children were very sad.

Fionnuala: We are heartbroken.

Aodh: We have no one to love us anymore.

Fiachra: Nobody comes to visit us anymore.

Con: We no longer sing and dance.

Fionn: Three hundred years have passed. It is time to go to the sea of Moyle.

Narrator 3: The swans flew to the sea. The sea was very rough, and time passed slowly.

Narrator 1: Time moved on and they moved to the Isle of Gloria.

Con: At least it is warmer here.

Aodh: There is more food.

Fiachra: But we are still so lonely.

Narrator 2: One day, they heard a ringing sound.

Fionnula: What is that sound?

Con: It sounds like a church bell.

Aodh: Christianity has come to Ireland.

Fiachra: You know what that means.

Narrator 3: An old man called Caomhog walked by the water.

Caomhóg: Who is talking? It can't be those swans.

Swans: Yes, it is us.

Caomhóg: How is that possible? Who are you?

Fionnuala: We are the children of Lir.

Con: Nine hundred years ago, our evil stepmother and Druid put a terrible spell on us.

Aodh: They turned us into swans.

Fiachra: They told us only a church bell ringing would break the spell.

Caomhog: Well, listen carefully. Can you hear it?

Swans: Yes.

Caomhóg: It is the church bell. Christianity has come to Ireland. *(He sprinkles holy water on them.)*

Narrator 1: Suddenly, the swans started to change back into humans.

Fiachra: At last.

Con: We are no longer children.

Aodh: We are so old.

Fionnuala: We are over nine hundred years old.

Narrator 2: The children hugged each other and held hands and then they fell to the floor. They were dead.

Caomhóg: At last, they are on their way to heaven to be with their mother and father again.

(King and Queen come to greet them, and they hug each other at the end.)

The Beggarman

Characters: Two narrators, three Fenians, Fionn, warrior, Conán Maol, Beggarman.

Narrator 1: One summer's day the Fianna went hunting. *(Fionn, Conán Maol and the Fenians enter the stage. They are carrying spears.)*

Fenian 1: It is a good day for hunting.

Fenian 2: We should take all our camping gear.

Fenian 3: I know a good place on Howth Hill where we could set up camp for the night.

Conán Maol: I'm feeling fit today. I will run faster than any of you. *(He starts stretching and running on the spot.)*

Fianna: Ha ha. *(All the Fianna look at him in amusement.)*

Fenian 1: Don't be ridiculous; you are short and round.

Fenian 2: Well, you can try.

Narrator 2: The Fianna heard a strange noise from the bushes.

Narrator 1: An old beggarman appeared.

Beggarman: Fast, you run fast. I don't think so. No one can outrun me.

Narrator 2: Everyone stared at him in amazement.

Fionn: You can barely walk. Your boots are covered in old dried mud. *(The beggarman struggles to walk. He can barely lift his feet.)*

Narrator 2: A ship docked in the bay and a warrior jumped ashore.

(Enter a warrior. Nobody notices him because they are too busy looking at the beggar's boots. They suddenly notice him as he creeps up behind them.)

Fionn: Welcome. I'm Fionn, the leader of Fianna.

(He stretches out his hand to shake the warriors hand, but the warrior points the sword at the Fianna.)

Warrior: I challenge your fastest runner to a race.

Fionn: Challenge accepted. What is the prize?

Warrior: All the gold horses and chariots in Ireland.

Fionn: *(points to the beggarman)* He is our fastest runner.

Beggarman: I accept your offer. We shall ride sixty miles on horses today and race back to this spot in the morning.

Fenian 1: Why is Fionn letting this happen?

Conán Maol: Even I'm faster than him.

Narrator 1: The warrior and the beggarman rode sixty miles.

Narrator 2: It was late when they bedded down for the night.

Narrator 1: The next morning, the warrior was keen to start the race.

Narrator 2: He tried to wake up the beggarman.

Warrior: Wake up, beggarman. We must begin the race.

Beggarman: It is far too early to run. If you are in a hurry, you can go, and I will follow.

Narrator 1: Finally, the beggarman woke up.

Beggarman: I better catch this warrior.

Narrator 2: With a hop, skip and a jump, the beggarman caught up with the warrior.

(Warrior looks shocked.)

Beggarman: Have you stopped for lunch yet?

Warrior: I'm too busy winning this race.

Beggarman: Well, I'm hungry.

Narrator 1: With another hop, skip and jump, he was well head of the warrior.

Beggarman: What lovely juicy blackberries. I will have them for my lunch.

(Finally, the warrior appears.)

Warrior: The tails of your coat are caught in the bush ten miles behind.

Beggarman: I better go back and get them

Warrior: That got rid of him.

Narrator 1: The beggarman took two hops back and collected his tails and took three long hops and a jump, and he was ahead of the warrior once more.

(Meanwhile, on Howth Hill, Fionn and the Fianna were waiting.)

Fenian 1: Does anyone see them?

Fenian 2: What's that in the distance?

Fenian 3: I don't believe it. It is the beggarman.

Conán Maol: He has reached here first.

Fionn: Thank you, beggarman. You have saved the honour of the Fianna.

Beggarman: You're welcome. I've enjoyed my time with you; now, I must return home.

(Suddenly, there was a white mist and the beggarman disappeared.)

Fenian 1: How did you know he would beat the warrior?

Fionn: Appearances are deceptive. That wasn't a beggarman. It was the prince of Tir na n-Óg. Once a year, he becomes human. Now, he has gone back to the land of the young.

(They all wave at the white mist.)

Fionn and the Giant

Characters: Narrator, Una, Giant, Fionn/baby.

Narrator: Fionn mac Cumhaill lived with his wife Una by the sea in Antrim. One day, Una was at home. She was sweeping the floor when she heard thunderous footsteps.

Una: *(stops sweeping)* Oh my goodness. Who is making all that noise?

Narrator: There was a loud knock at the door. There was an enormous giant standing at the door.

Una: Who are you? What do you want?

Giant: I'm Angus. I'm the tallest, strongest and scariest giant in the whole of the isle of Scotland. I'm here to challenge Fionn to a duel.

Una: Well, I'm Una, Fionn's wife. *(She puts out her hand.)* I'm very pleased to meet you.

Giant: It is a pleasure to meet you.

Una: Scotland is a long way off. How did you get here? Did you come by boat?

Giant: No. I made a pathway of stones across the sea. Is Fionn here?

Una: He is gone hunting. I don't think he was expecting you. You are more than welcome to come in and wait for him. He should be back soon.

Giant: That's very kind of you. Thank you.

Una: Sit by the fire and I'll make you a cup of tea. How do you like it?

Giant: Milk and two sugars.

Una: Could you speak a little softer because I only got the baby to sleep.

Giant: Of course. *(Una gives him the tea and they both sit by the fire.)*

Baby: *(Crying.)*

Giant: The baby is crying.

Una: He must be hungry again. Would you like to see him?

Giant: I love babies. Of course I would. *(He looks at the baby.)*

Giant: How old is the baby? He is very big.

Una: He is only a month old.

Giant: But he must be two meters.

Una: He is two and half metres tall.

Giant: If this is Fionn's son, how tall is Fionn?

Una: Don't you know? Fionn is enormous. He is twice your size and you aren't small.

Giant: He has a fine set of teeth and he has a beard.

Una: He is very hairy for a baby. I must shave him twice a day.

Giant: I think fighting Fionn may not be such a clever idea. I think it's time to leave. I must be off.

Una: Oh, please don't leave. Fionn will be disappointed he missed you.

Giant: I must go. I just remembered I told my wife I would be home for dinner. We are having haggis tonight. It's my favourite.

Una: What a pity. Goodbye. It was nice meeting you.

Giant: *(Jumps on the stones.)* What if Fionn decides to follow me. I will take the stones with me as I go so he can't reach me. *(He starts picking up the stones as he goes.)*

Una: You can come out now. He's gone.

Fionn/Baby: Our trick worked. The baby was me.

Narrator: Angus the Scottish giant was never seen again.

Saint Patrick

Characters: Three narrators, three slave traders, Patrick, Patrick's mother, Patrick's father, a rich Merchant, three sheep, God, the ship's captain, three druids, High King, snakes (as many as you want)

Narrator 1: Once upon a time in the north of France, there lived a young boy called Patrick.

Narrator 2: Patrick was young and carefree. He lived in a village with his family and friends.

Narrator 3: One night while the whole village was fast asleep, the village was raided by evil slave traders.

(Patrick and his parents are asleep. Slave traders enter the stage very quietly. They have their swords drawn.)

Slave Trader 1: Take any valuables you can lay your hands on.

Slave Trader 2: The only thing of value in this village is this young boy.

Slave Trader 3: Yes, he is young and hearty; he will make an excellent slave.

Slave Trader 1: Seize him.

Slave Trader 2: And leave the rest. They are of no use.

(Slave Traders 1 and 2 tie up Patrick's parents.)

Patrick's Mother: Please don't take our son. He is our only child.

Slave Trader 3: Silence woman.

Patrick's Father: Where are you taking him?

Slave Trader 1: We are going to sail to Ireland.

Patrick's Father: What are you going to do with him in Ireland?

Slave Trader 2: We will sell him at the market.

Slave Trader 3: People will pay good money for a strong and fit slave.

Slave Trader 1: And there is nothing you can do about it.

Narrator 1: That very night, the slave traders and the boy set sail for Ireland.

Narrator 2: Patrick was very frightened because he had only ever known a comfortable and safe life with his family in the north of France.

Patrick: I'm so scared. I've never been anywhere by myself before.

Narrator 3: Eventually, they arrived in Ireland, and the slave traders sold him to a rich merchant.

Rich Merchant: He looks very hearty and strong. I will be able to work him hard. How much do you want for this boy?

Slave Traders: Five pieces of silver.

Rich Merchant: 1, 2, 3, 4, 5. Boy, come with me.

Patrick: Where are we going?

Rich Merchant: You are going to work as a shepherd. You must take care of my sheep on the mountain. You can live in this stone hut. Now, get to work.

Patrick: I know nothing about sheep.

Rich Merchant: I paid good money for you, so you must keep the flock safe. Make sure none of them run off or get injured.

Narrator 1: Patrick worked very hard on the mountain. Soon, he became good friends with the sheep as they were his only company. *(Patrick sits on a rock and looks very sad.)*

Sheep 1: Baa, baa what's the matter, Patrick?

Sheep 2: You always look sad.

Patrick: I miss my family and friends very much. I want to go home.

Sheep 3: I've an idea that could help.

Patrick: What is it? I'll try anything that will help me return to my family.

Sheep 3: Ask God to help you escape and return you safely to your family.

Patrick: That's an excellent plan. *(He kneels.)* God, please help me escape so I can return to my family in the north of France. *(He waits for a response but there is none.)* Nothing, I guess I'm stuck here.

Sheep: Be patient. God works in mysterious ways,

Narrator 2: In the seventh winter, Patrick was fast asleep in his hut one night when God came to him.

God: It's time to leave the mountain and return to your family, friends and village. There is a ship in Wexford waiting for you.

Patrick: *(wakes up)* God, that's a very dangerous plan. If I get caught, I'll surely die.

God: Well, just make sure you don't get caught.

Sheep 1: You must go.

Sheep 2: God has spoken.

Sheep 3: We will miss you.

Patrick: I'll miss you too, but I need to return home.

Sheep: Go quickly, bye and safe journey.

(They all hug.)

Patrick: Bye and take care.

Narrator 1: Patrick trekked through the mountains. It began to snow. He was cold and hungry.

(Musics plays as Patrick mimes going through the treacherous terrains.)

Narrator 2: He arrived in Wexford just as a big ship was to set sail.

Ship's captain: All aboard.

Patrick: Where are you going, Captain?

Ship's Captain: The north of France. Hop on if you want a ride.

Narrator 3: After many days, Patrick arrived home. *(His parents are busying working in the fields. They notice someone walking towards. They look carefully and realise it is their long, lost son.)*

Patrick's Mother: You are home. I'm so happy to see you.

Patrick's Father: I prayed to God every day for seven years for your safe return.

(They all hug each other.)

Patrick: I'll never leave you again.

Narrator 1: It's few years later, and Patrick is sleeping.

God: Patrick, I need you to return to Ireland and tell the people all about me and Christianity.

Narrator 2: Before he returned to Ireland, he became a monk.

Narrator 3: And then a bishop. And in 432, he returned to Ireland to tell the people about God and Christianity. *(He puts on a bishop's hat.)*

Narrator 1: Patrick arrived carrying the Christian cross. The pagan druids of Ireland were not impressed.

Druid 1: What do you want with your funny ideas and your big cross?

Patrick: I've come to tell you to stop worshiping your pagan gods. There is only one God, and he is three people: the Father, Son and Holy Ghost.

Druid 2: We should get rid of him.

Druid 1: He doesn't agree with our pagan rituals.

Druid 2: Three people in one God? That makes no sense.

Druid 3: He is a ridiculous person.

Druid 1: How are you going to explain your God to our people?

(Patrick looks around and picks up a shamrock)

Patrick: I'll explain it. One shamrock, Three leaves. One God, three people.

Druid 2: We have many gods, and they aren't stuck in one person.

High King: Stop this nonsense at once. Patrick, you are free to believe in whatever God you wish. Travel the land and spread the word. However, I think it will be a hard sell.

Narrator 1: Patrick travelled the country and when he reached Mayo, he decided ….

Patrick: I will spend 40 days and 40 nights alone on this mountain, praying to God.

Narrator 2: While he was on the mountain top, he realised there were lots of snakes. They started to surround him.

Snakes: Hisssssssssssssssssssssss.

Patrick: These snakes are annoying and dangerous.

God: Banish all the serpents to the sea.

Druids and High King: Did you see that?

Patrick: All the snakes are gone.

Druid 1: I'm converting to this religion with one God with three divine people.

Druid 2: Me too.

Druid 3: Me too.

High King: You shouldn't have judged so quickly.

Narrator 2: Word spread, and all of Ireland became Christian.

Patrick: Mission accomplished at last.

Narrator 1: Since that day, there has never been a snake seen in Ireland.

Narrator 2: Patrick stayed in Ireland and he died on the 17th March 461.

Narrator 3: Since then, the 17th March has been St Patrick's Day.

Queen Maebh

Characters: Two narrators, High King, Maebh, Conor, King of Ulster, Eithne, Furbaide, Tinni Mac Conri, Ailill Mac Máta, Fergus Mac Roich, Druid, Servant, Messenger, Red Branch Knights (as many as you want.), Queen Maebh's army (as many as you want.)

Narrator 1: Once upon a time, Eochaidh Feidleach was High King of Ireland.

Narrator 2: Eochaidh Feidleach had a daughter called Maebh.

(Enter King and Maebh on stage.)

High King: Maebh, clean your room.

Maebh: No, I will not clean my room. *(Folds arm and stamps her foot.)* Isn't that what servants are for?

High King: Don't be so rude. I'm the High King of Ireland. You should have more respect.

Maebh: Whatever.

(Enter messenger.)

Messenger: I've important news for Conor, King of Ulster.

High King: What does he want?

Messenger: He wants a wife and he thinks Maebh, who is renowned throughout the land for her beauty, would be ideal.

High King: *(He addressed the audience.)* If I marry her off to Conor, King of Ulster, I would finally get rid of her. She would be off my hands forever. Now, I must appear to be enthusiastic. *(He turns to the messenger.)*

High King: Well, tell Conor, King of Ulster, I will consider his proposal. Mmmmm, I've thought about it. He can have her. *(The king pushes Maebh towards the messenger.)*

(Messenger looks confused.)

High King: Tell him he can marry Maebh tomorrow. Here, take her with you.

Maebh: Where am I going?

High King: Go with this nice man. He will take you to your new home.

Maebh: I don't want a new home. I'm happy here with you.

High King: You will never have to clean your room again.

(Messenger takes Maebh by the hand and they leave the stage.)

(King is delighted and does a jig off stage.)

Narrator 1: Soon they were married.

(Conor and Maebh walk down the aisle hand in hand as wedding bells ring in the background.)

Narrator 2: Soon, they had a son called Glaisne.

(Maebh walks on the stage with the baby. Conor follows close behind her.)

Maebh: I'm so miserable. Conor is a terrible husband. He is so controlling, and he is always in a bad mood.

Conor: I'm bad-tempered? You are the worst wife in the whole wide world.

Maebh: Well, if that's what you think of me, I'm off for home to my father.

(Maebh storms off to her father's house. She knocks hard on the door.)

High King: Hold your horses, I'm coming. Hello, what are you doing here?

Maebh: I'm back. I wished I had never married Conor, King of Ulster. And do you know who I blame for my disaster of a marriage?

High King: Who?

Maebh: You.

(She storms off with her baby and leaves her suitcase for the king to pick up.)

High King: This is not good news. Conor will blame me. What shall I do? I know—Eithne, come here at once.

Eithne: Yes Father, whatever is the matter?

High King: Maebh is back, and she isn't happy.

Eithne: Oh dear. I was enjoying the quiet.

High King: I need you to be nice and keep the peace.

Eithne: I'm always nice.

Narrator 1: Eithne married Conor. They had a child called Furbaide. They were very happy together.

(Eithne and Conor walk on the stage together. Maebh looks at them in anger.)

Maebh: I don't believe this. She knows how badly he treated me and now she is playing happy families with him. Servant, come here.

Servant: Yes, your majesty

Maebh: Go to Conor, King of Ulster's castle and kill Queen Eithne.

(She hands him a dagger. Eithne is killed off stage. High King walks slowly on to the stage. He is upset but gets angry when he sees Maebh.)

High King: How could you have murdered your sister? I'm sending you to Connaught to marry the king. It will keep you out of danger because Conor will want to seek his revenge. No matter how cruel you have been, I can't lose another daughter. Now go.

Narrator 1: She married Tinni Mac Conri. They were happy for a while, but she fell in love with another man: Ailill Mac Máta. Tinni became very jealous.

Tinni: I challenge you to a duel.

Ailill: The winner wins your wife.

(Tinni and Ailill mime a sword fight. Tinni loses and falls to the floor and dies.)

Narrator 2: After a fierce duel, Tinni lost and died a slow and painful death. *(Maebh walks over Tinni's dead body.)*

Ailill: Maebh, will you marry me? *(He gets down on one knee.)*

Maebh: My hero. Yes, of course I will marry you. *(They hug.)*

Narrator 1: They were very happy, and they had seven children, but Maebh still wanted Conor, King of Ulster, to suffer.

Maebh: I want someone to kill Connor, King of Ulster.

(Fergus walks past her. He hears her and stops.)

Fergus: I'm sorry, but I couldn't help overhearing you. Did you mention Conor, King of Ulster?

Maebh: Yes, I did. I want him dead.

Fergus: Well, today is your lucky day. I'm Fergus Mac Roich, an Ulster warrior. It just so happens Conor banished me from Ulster, and that's why I've moved to Connaught.

Maebh: If you hate Conor as much as me, then you will help our army defeat the Ulster army.

Narrator 2: Maebh declared war on Ulster but decided the only way she could win was if she played a trick on Conor and his army.

Maebh: Druid, come here at once.

Druid: Yes, Your Majesty. *(He bows before her.)*

Maebh: I want you to put a spell on Conor's army, the red branch knights.

Druid: I have a plan. I could spread this sleep dust and make everyone fall asleep.

(He spreads the sleep dust. One by one, the red branch knights yawn loudly and fall to the ground with a thump.)

Narrator 1: The only one who managed to stay awake was the mighty Cúchulainn, Conor's nephew.

(He staggers on to the stage, yawns, shakes his head and wakes up fully.)

Cúchulainn: I'm the greatest fighter who ever walked this land. I can take on Queen Maebh and her army.

(A sword fight ensues and Cúchulainn kills all the army except for Fergus.)

Maebh: Kill him, Fergus, kill him.

Fergus: I refuse. Cúchulainn is my godson.

Maebh: Coward.

Fergus: I'm not a coward.

Maebh: Prove it.

(Fergus and Cúchulainn continue their sword fight until they both die.)

Maebh: Oh well, it's time to go home. *(Steps over all the dead bodies and starts to walk off the stage.)*

(Furbaide enters the stage and is appalled by all the dead bodies.)

Furbaide: This woman causes death and destruction wherever she goes. Well, not anymore.

(Furbaide picks up his sling and a rock.)

Furbaide: Beautiful Queen Maebh, please turn around.

(Maebh turns around and Furbaide fires the sling; the rock hits her and she dies instantly.)

Furbaide: Queen Maebh will cause no more bloodshed.

FIONN AND THE DRAGON

Characters: Two narrators, Fionn, Finéigeas, High King, Goll Mac Morna, Stranger, Two magicians, two warriors, Dragon, people at the banquet.

Fionn: I'm going to the Great Festival of Samhain to see the High King.

Finéigeas: Well, enjoy yourself. I hope you have an enjoyable time.

Narrator: Fionn walked all day and eventually arrived at the great banqueting hall at Tara.

(They are lots of people sitting at tables. Enter the High King.)

High King: Who are you? I don't think I've had the pleasure.

Fionn: I'm Fionn, the son of Cumhaill.

High King: You are my friend's son. You are welcome to my humble castle. *(They hug.)* Come take a seat.

Narrator 2: What Fionn didn't know was that the man who killed his father, Goll Mac Marna, was enjoying the feast

Goll Mac Morna: I hope Fionn doesn't recognize me. I killed his father so I would become leader of the Fianna. *(He hides under the table.)*

Narrator 1: Everyone enjoyed the feast.

High King: Everyone, I hope you are enjoying the feast. Unfortunately, we have a very big threat to Tara.

Fionn: What's the threat?

High King: Every year, Tara is visited by a fire-breathing dragon that causes lots of damage.

Fionn: Can you not do something? You have great warriors.

Warrior 1: We have tried everything, and we failed miserably.

Warrior 2: We have given up.

Fionn: Can your great magicians not put a spell on him?

Magician 1: We have tried every spell in our spell book.

Magician 2: We have failed miserably. Fionn, maybe you can help us?

Fionn: What do I need to do?

High King: Defend Tara from the evil dragon.

Narrator 1: Fionn left the banquet.

Fionn: How will I defend Tara from the dragon? I hear footsteps behind me. Someone is following me.

Fionn: Who goes there?

Stranger: I was a friend of your father. I want to help you.

Fionn: Why do you want to help me?

Stranger: Your father helped me once. I want to return the favour.

Fionn: Well, I'll take all the help I can get.

Stranger: Listen carefully to me. When the dragon approaches you, he plays sweet music. Anyone who hears the music will fall into a deep sleep.

Fionn: What shall I do?

Stranger: Take this spear and as soon as you hear the sweet music, press it against your head and the music will lose its power.

(Dragon enters.)

Dragon: It's that time of year again. I'm off to Tara to wreak havoc on the High King and his subjects.

Narrator 1: The music started to play and all the people in Tara fell asleep one by one.

(Music starts playing. All the subjects start yawning and they fall asleep.)

Fionn: I hear the music. I'll press the spear against my head and I'll remain awake.

Dragon: My work is nearly done. Everyone is asleep except for this man. I'll breathe flames on him, and that will teach him a lesson.

Narrator 2: So, the dragon breathed a long blue flame.

Fionn: Here comes the great blue flame. I'll fire the spear at him.

Narrator 1: Fionn aimed and fired the spear. The spear pierced the dragon's heart.

Dragon: What happened? Oh dear, I'm dying.

Fionn: Dragon, that will teach you not to frighten everyone in Tara. You never will be able frighten anyone ever again.

High King: You are a hero. As a reward, I will grant you a wish.

Fionn: I want to be the leader of the Fianna, like my father.

High King: Goll Mac Morna, you must accept Fionn as the leader of Fianna or else I will banish you from this fair land.

Goll Mac Morna: I have never seen such bravery. I will gladly stand down and accept Fionn as the new leader of the Fianna.

(Fionn kneels before the High King. The High King puts his sword on both of Fionn's shoulders.)

High King: Rise, new leader of the Fianna. *(Fionn rises as the new leader of the Fianna.)*

The Story of Saint Brendan

Characters: Two narrators, Saint Brendan, four monks, Abbot. Jasconius, two whales, Christopher Columbus.

Narrator 1: Once upon a time, there lived a monk called Brendan.

Brendan: I'm Brendan the navigator. I've gone on many adventures, but now I'm old. I've one last trip in me.

Monk 1: Brendan, you are too old for adventures.

Brendan: You are never too old for an adventure, you know.

Monk 2: You are mad to plan this trip by yourself.

Monks 3: We can't let you go by yourself. We will come with you.

Monk 1 & 2: We will?

Monk 3: Yes, we can't let him go by himself.

Abbot: If you want to go on a voyage, then you have my blessing. Come, let's have one more meal together on land. *(They mime eating their last meal together.)*

Narrator 2: The next morning, the monks and Brendan walked to the shore. They came to the boat.

Monk 1: Is this the boat we are using?

Monk 2: It is a bit small, don't you think?

Monk 3: It doesn't seem very solid for such a long journey.

(The abbot hugs them all and waves goodbye.)

Abbot: Goodbye, everyone.

Brendan: The coast of Ireland is getting smaller and smaller. Now I can't even see it.

Monk 1: Look, there is an island.

Monk 2: It's covered in sheep.

Monk 3: It's just like home, then.

Brendan: We have discovered new land. Let's call it the Faroe Islands.

Narrator 1: They got off the boat.

Monk 1: We should light a fire on the beach.

Brendan: We should say mass.

Monk 2: The three of us will collect firewood.

Monk 3: Brendan, you stay here and prepare the mass.

(The monks go off to collect the firewood, Brendan is sitting on the beach.)

Brendan: What's that noise. It sounds like snoring. *(He gets up and walks along the beach.)*

Brendan: What's this? It is a type of animal that is half in and half out of the water.

Jasconius: I'm Jasconius the whale. You have woken me up. I'm having forty winks.

Brendan: I'm Brendan. I'm a monk. Pleased to meet you.

(The three monks return with firewood in their hands.)

Monk 1: Oh, my goodness. What is that large creature?

Monk 2: It is enormous. I think it's a whale.

Monk 3: Don't move, Brendan. We will protect you from the whale.

Brendan: Monks, do not fear this large and noble creature. This is my new friend, Jasconius the whale.

Jasconius: Hello, everyone. I must be off now, but I'll pass a message to all the whales in the sea to help you on your journey to the promised land.

Brendan: Thank you.

(The next day, Brendan and the monks took off to the promised land. They sailed away. A few days later, they came across some whales.)

Whale 1: Hello, Brendan. Jasconius told us to guide you to the promised land.

Whale 2: We are here to help you. *(The whales swim in front of the boat, protecting them from the dangerous elements in the sea.)*

Narrator 2: Eventually they arrived in the promised land of the saints.

Monks: We have reached our destination at last. Give praise to God. This is the promised land.

Brendan: It has taken seven years to get here. Now, I can die happily.

Narrator 1: Brendan lay down and fell asleep forever.

Narrator 2: Nine hundred years later, a man called Christopher Columbus arrived on the island.

Christopher Columbus: I've been sailing for years to get here. I shall call this land America.

The Clever Leprechaun and His Pot of Gold

Characters: Narrator, Old Man, Leprechaun.

Narrator: One night, an old man was walking home from the pub in the village.

Old Man: What a beautiful night it is tonight. The moon is shining brightly in the sky.

(A leprechaun is sitting near the bushes with his crock of gold. He is counting his gold coins.)

Leprechaun: 2005, 2006, 2007. I hear someone coming. I better bury my gold underneath this bush.

(He quickly buries his pot of gold.)

Old Man: What's the noise? *(He stops and listens.)* It is coming from over there. Hello. Is there anyone there?

Narrator: The old man couldn't believe his eyes. In front of him stood a leprechaun. *(The old man grabbed the leprechaun.)*

Old Man: Oh, my goodness, you can't possibly be a ….

Leprechaun: Yes, I'm a leprechaun. Now put me down at once.

Old Man: Not so fast. Finding a leprechaun is like winning the lottery. Every leprechaun has a pot of gold hidden somewhere.

Leprechaun: Let me go.

Old Man: If you want me to let you go, take me to your pot of gold.

Leprechaun: Let me go and I'll show you where I buried the pot of gold. Come with me. *(He points to a bush.)* I buried it underneath this bush.

Old Man: I need to go home and get a shovel.

Leprechaun: Off you go.

Old Man: Wait, how will I know where the gold is buried? All these bushes look the same.

Leprechaun: Do you have a handkerchief?

Old Man: I have this bright red one.

Leprechaun: Mark the bush with your handkerchief so when you come back, you will know where the gold is.

Old Man: What a clever idea. Thank you, Leprechaun.

Narrator: The old man ran home, grabbed his shovel and ran back to the bush as quick as he could. The leprechaun had left him a very big surprise.

Old Man: Every bush here has a red handkerchief tied to them. How will I know which bush has the gold underneath it? The leprechaun fooled me. I will never be rich.

Narrator: The old man hobbled home. He was very disappointed.

Leprechaun: Ha, ha, that taught him a lesson. Never trust a leprechaun.

TIR NA N-ÓG

Characters: Two narrators, Fionn, Oisín, Niamh, King, Queen, horse, two men, a wise man.

Narrator 1: One day, Fionn and his son Oisín were hunting on the shores of Loch Léin.

Fionn: I'm real pleased with the fat juicy deer we caught today.

Oisín: We will eat well tonight.

Fionn: Do you hear something?

Oisín: It sounds like a galloping horse.

Narrator 2: Soon, they saw a woman with long golden hair on a white horse galloping towards them in the distance.

Oisín: She is the most beautiful woman I have ever laid my eyes on.

(The woman sees them and comes to a halt.)

Fionn: Hello, I'm Fionn, leader of the Fianna. Who are you?

Niamh: I'm Niamh of the Golden Hair. My father is the king of a land called Tir na Óg.

Fionn: I'm very pleased to meet you. *(He shakes her hand.)* Welcome to our fair land. How may I help you?

Niamh: I am looking for a warrior called Oisín.

Fionn: You are in luck. This is my son, the warrior Oisín. *(He pushes Oisín in front of him. Oisín is in awe of her beauty.)*

Oisín: Pleased to meet you. What does a beautiful woman like you want with me?

Niamh: I heard you are a very brave warrior and you write the most amazing poetry, I would really like if you came back to Tir na Óg with me.

Oisín: I have never heard of this land. What is like?

Niamh: It is the land of the young. It so beautiful. It is a land without pain; it is a place where all your dreams come true and no one is sad. No one ever grows old in Tir na Óg.

Oisín: You don't have to ask me twice. It sounds amazing. *(He jumps on to the horse with Niamh.)*

Fionn: Enjoy yourself. Have a wonderful time.

Oisín: Bye, Father. I'll come back soon to tell you of my wonderful adventures.

Narrator 1: Niamh and Oisín galloped off over the loch. Soon, they arrived in Tir na n-Óg.

King: Welcome to Tir na n-Óg.

Queen: May you be very happy here with our beautiful daughter.

Narrator 2: Fionn had a wonderful time. He hunted and fished. He loved spending time with Niamh; however, he did miss his father and the Fianna.

Oisín: I think it's time I went back home to visit my family.

Niamh: Are you not happy here?

Oisín: Yes, I am, but I long to see my family.

Niamh: I don't want you to go but I want you to be happy. Take my horse. It knows the way to Ireland. You must promise me one thing.

Oisín: Anything.

Niamh: You are not to get off the horse or let your foot touch the ground.

Oisín: I promise.

Narrator 1: So, Oisín said his goodbyes and jumped on the horse and galloped off to Ireland. *(He hugs Niamh and her parents and jumps on the horse.)*

King: Did you tell him not to touch the soil in Ireland?

Niamh: Yes, of course.

Queen: Did you tell him why?

Niamh: No, he doesn't need to know the reason.

Oisín: At last I'm back in Ireland. It has changed a lot in the few years I've been away. Nothing looks familiar.

Narrator 1: Soon, he passed some men trying to move a rock.

Man 1: Heave.

Man 2: You need to push harder.

Man 1: I'm doing my best.

Man 2: Look, there is a man on a horse. He looks strong; he might be able to help.

Man 1: Excuse me, could you help us move this rock?

Oisín: Of course, I can.

Narrator 2: He bent down and moved the rock with one hand.

Man 2: I told you he looked strong.

Narrator 1: Just then, Oisín lost his balance and fell to the ground. The moment he touched the ground, he turned into an old man, and the white horse galloped off and left him.

Man 1: What has happened to the young strong man?

Oisín: I don't know what has happened. Please help me?

Man 2: We can ask the wise man to help us. *(Men run off and bring back the wise man.)*

Wise Man: Who are you?

Oisín: I'm Oisín, son of Fionn, the leader of the Fianna. Can you get him for me? I would be very grateful.

Wise man: I'm sorry. Fionn has been dead for over three hundred years. There is a legend that Fionn's son went to the land of Tír na n-Óg and married a beautiful girl with golden hair.

Oisín: That's me.

Wise Man: If that is true, you must be over three hundred years old.

Oisín: I haven't been away from Ireland for a few years but for over three hundred years. No wonder I'm so old.

Narrator 2: Oisín closed his eyes and died.

Narrator 1: The white horse returned to Tír na n-Óg alone.

(Niamh is seen crying when she realises Oisín isn't going to return.)

Pronunciation of Irish Words:

Ailill: Al/ill
Aodh: Aay
Aoife: E/fa
Caomhóg: Kwee/vogue
Conán Maol: Co/nan Mw/ale
Connacht: Konn/uckt
Cúchulainn: Koo/Kul/in
Eithne: Eth/na
Eochaid: Ucky
Feidleach: Fed/lock
Furbaide: Fur/bade
Fiachra: Feee/ack/ra
Fianna: Fee/an/ah
Finéigeas: Fin/e/gas
Fionn: Fe/on
Fionnuala: Fin/new/la
Howth: Hoath
Lir: Leer
Mac: Mock

Máta: Maw/ta
Maebh: May/v
Niamh: Knee/uv
Oisín: Ush/een
Roich: Row/ick
Samhain: Sow/in
Tir na n-Óg: Tear/na/knogue
Una: Oo/na

Other Books by the Author:

Drama Start Series:

Drama Start: Drama Activities, Plays and Monologues for Children (Ages 3-8)

Drama Start Two: Drama Activities for Children (Ages 9-12)

Stage Start: 20 Plays for Children (Ages 3-12)

Stage Start Two: 20 More Plays for Children (Ages 3-12)

Movement Start: Over 100 Movement Activities and Stories for Children

ESL Drama Start: Drama Activities and Plays for ESL Learners

On Stage Series:

Fairytales on Stage: A Collection of Plays for Children

Classics on Stage: A Collection of Plays Based on Classic Children's Stories

Aesop's Fables on Stage: A Collection of Plays Based on Aesop's Fables

Christmas Stories on Stage: A Collection of Plays for Children

Panchatantra on Stage: A Collection of Plays for Children

Hans Christian Andersen's Stories on Stage: A Collection of Plays for Children

Oscar Wilde's Stories on Stage: A Collection of Plays based on Oscar Wilde's Short Stories

Just so Stories on Stage: A Collection of Plays based on Rudyard Kipling's Just so Stories

Animal Stories on Stage: A Collection of Plays based on Animal Stories

More Fairytales on Stage: A Collection Plays for Children based on Fairytales

www.ingramcontent.com/pod-product-compliance
Lightning Source LLC
Chambersburg PA
CBHW071226020526
44118CB00036BA/2141